KU-178-132

SEND IN THE CLONES

Three plays

by Steve Barlow and Steve Skidmore

Series Editors: Steve Barlow and Steve Skidmore

Published by Heinemann Educational Publishers
Halley Court, Jordan Hill, Oxford OX2 8EJ
A division of Reed Educational and Professional Publishing Ltd

OXFORD MELBOURNE AUCKLAND
JOHANNESBURG BLANTYRE GABORONE
IBADAN PORTSMOUTH (NH) USA CHICAGO

© Steve Barlow and Steve Skidmore, 2002

All rights reserved. No part of this publication may be reproduced in any material form
(including photocopying or storing it in any medium by electronic means and whether
or not transiently or incidentally to some other use of this publication) without the prior
written permission of the copyright owner, except in accordance with the provisions of
the Copyright, Designs and Patents Act 1988 or under the terms of a licence issued by
the Copyright Licensing Agency Ltd, 90 Tottenham Court Road, London W1P 0LP.
Applications for the copyright owner's written permission to reproduce any part of this
publication should be addressed in the first instance to the publisher.

First published 2002

06 05 04 03 02
10 9 8 7 6 5 4 3 2 1

ISBN 0 435 21452 7

Illustrations by Andrew Skilleter
Cover design by Shireen Nathoo Design
Designed and typeset by Artistix, Thame, Oxon
Printed and bound in Great Britain by Biddles Ltd

Tel: 01865 888058 www.heinemann.co.uk

Contents

All the plays are set in the year 2035

Note: when these plays are performed, it's unlikely that the actors playing the clones will look exactly alike. But they might wear transparent half-masks, and if they are dressed alike, and have similar hairstyles, the point will be made. It will also help if the clones have similar ways of moving, smiling etc. Mirror-movement exercises will help to develop these habits.

Double Trouble: characters

MICK

MIKE

JESS

JESSICA

DOUBLE TROUBLE

The Air Bar. It doesn't sell drinks, it sells canisters of oxygen. Mike is sitting at a table. He is waiting nervously. Mick enters. He looks exactly the same as Mike. (They are clones.)

MICK:	Hi Mike!
MIKE:	Hi Mick! What are you doing here?
MICK:	I've got a date.

MIKE:	Spooky! So have I. *(He sits down next to Mick)* Where did you meet her?
MICK:	I haven't met her yet. It's a blind date.
MIKE:	Even spookier! I'm on a blind date too. I joined a computer dating agency.
MICK:	I don't believe it! So did I. Which dating agency did you use?
MIKE:	Lonely Clones.
MICK:	Amazing! That's the one I used. Do you think that all clones act in the same way? Is it something in the genes?
MIKE:	It can't be, I'm wearing trousers.
MICK:	*(Not amused)* Ho ho. Don't bother telling your date any jokes, or she won't be your date any longer.
MIKE:	Don't worry, she'll be turned on by my good looks.
MICK:	I'll agree that you're good looking! Just like me!
	(They both laugh.)
MIKE:	I'm impressed with the dating agency. My date is beautiful.
MICK:	So is mine. I can't wait to meet her.
	(Jessica walks in. She looks around. Mick and Mike see her. Their jaws drop.)

MICK:	Wow! That girl is drop-dead gorgeous.
MIKE:	Yeah! And the great thing is – she's my date!
MICK:	What do you mean she's your date? She's my date!
MIKE:	No way! I'll show you her picture.
	(Mike shows Mick his mobile phone-computer. He punches a few keys.)
MIKE:	See! Jessica Smith. Meet at the Air Bar, Tuesday, seven o'clock. My date.
	(Mick pulls out his mobile phone-computer. He also punches a few keys. Then he shows Mike.)
MICK:	Jessica Smith. Meet at the Air Bar, Tuesday, seven o'clock. My date.
MIKE:	Oh no! The agency must have mixed us up! We've both been given the same date. What are we going to do?
MICK:	I was here first, so she's mine.
MIKE:	No way, I saw her first!
	(Jessica spots Mike and Mick. She walks over and stares at them.)
JESSICA:	Excuse me, I'm supposed to be meeting a Michael Ringer.
MICK/MIKE:	*(Together)* That's me!

(Jessica looks confused.)

MICK: We're both called Michael Ringer. We're clones.

JESSICA: Oh! I thought you looked alike.

MICK: Yeah, we're a couple of dead ringers. *(To Mike)* And you *will* be dead, if you don't lay off my date. *(To Jessica)* I'm known as Mick.

MIKE: And I'm known as Mike.

JESSICA: Oh. The agency must have got confused. They obviously didn't double-check.

MICK: Double-check. That's very funny. Ha, ha, ha…

MIKE: Yeah, double-check, brilliant! Ha, ha, ha…

(They are over-the-top laughing. Jessica doesn't get the joke. She just stares at them.)

MICK: *(Stops laughing)* Yeah well, I suppose it wasn't that funny.

MIKE: No, I suppose it wasn't…

(Jessica sits between Mick and Mike. There is an awkward pause.)

JESSICA: The air is very bad outside.

MICK: Is it?

JESSICA: Yes. Very high air pollution.

(Another pause.)

JESSICA: They say the oxygen is very good here.

MICK/MIKE: *(Together)* It is.

(Another pause.)

JESSICA: I'm dying for a gasp of air.

(Mick and Mike suddenly get the hint.)

MICK/MIKE: *(Together)* I'll get it! *(They glare at each other)*

MICK: *(Hissing under his breath)* I saw her first, I'll get it…

JESSICA: *(To Mick)* Why don't you get the first shot, then Mike can get the next.

MIKE: Good idea. I'll have my oxygen with a drop of carbon dioxide. I like it fizzy.

JESSICA: I like mine still…

MIKE: Oh yeah, so do I. Cancel the bubbles, Mick.

MICK: Good idea, you're already full of air.

(Mick goes off to order the air.)

JESSICA: How long have you two known each other?

MIKE: Since we were in the same test tube.

JESSICA: He seems nice.

MIKE: *(Laughs)* Looks are deceiving! He might be incredibly good looking, but he's got some really bad habits. He picks his nose all the time and doesn't wash his feet. He even collects his belly button fluff and keeps it in a jar.

JESSICA:	How do you know?
MIKE:	'Cos I do the same… I mean, he told me. He tells me everything. We're like twins, but twins who are the same person.
JESSICA:	Right…
	(There is a pause. Mike decides to change the subject.)
MIKE:	You've got beautiful eyes, Jessica. They're really … green. Like cabbages.
JESSICA:	Cabbages!
MIKE:	No! I mean, like grass, no, I mean… They're lovely.
	(Mick returns.)
MICK:	He's not boring you, is he? He usually talks double-dutch.
	(They pick up the air masks that Mick has bought and take deep breaths.)
MICK:	*(To Mike)* Your turn to get them in. Repeat order.
	(Mike goes to order more gas.)
MICK:	You want to watch Mike. He's got some really bad habits.
JESSICA:	You mean he picks his nose, doesn't wash his feet and collects belly button fluff?
MICK:	*(A bit shaken)* Yeah. Good guess.

(There is a pause. Mick decides to change the subject.)

MICK: Has anyone told you, you've got beautiful eyes?

JESSICA: Funny you should ask that…

MICK: They're really… green.

JESSICA: Like cabbages?

MICK: That's right! They're like cabbages. *(He realises what he has said)* I mean, like grass… No, I mean, they're lovely.

(Mike returns.)

MIKE: I hope he's not boring you, Jessica. He has a habit of repeating himself.

JESSICA: No, he's not been repeating *himself.*

(They take the air. Jessica gets up.)

JESSICA: My turn to get the shots in. Same again? *(She goes to the bar)*

MICK: *(To Mike)* Listen, you double-crossing double. I bet you found out about my date and came here just to stop me. Leave her alone. She's mine.

MIKE: No way, you big clone. She's mine!

(Jess walks in. She is identical to Jessica. But she is dressed in more daring clothes – shorter skirt and top, high-heeled boots. She looks into her mobile-computer, then heads over to Mick and Mike.)

JESS:	Hi! I'm looking for a Michael Ringer.
MIKE/MICK:	*(Together – shocked)* We're both him!
JESS:	Thank goodness. I thought I'd had too much air and I was seeing double! I'm supposed to be on a date. Lonely Clones arranged it.
MIKE:	I'm Mike and he's Mick.
JESS:	Lonely Clones are always getting things wrong! Ah well, it doesn't matter. We can get a quick shot of air and then head to the robo rave. Spend the night dancing … and cloning around! I'll get us some air. In fact, I'll get doubles!
	(They all laugh. Jess has got a sense of humour. She goes to get the air.)
MIKE:	She's mine.
MICK:	No way. You wanted Jessica to be your date.
MIKE:	But I hadn't seen Jess. She's more fun. Jessica's boring.
	(Jessica returns.)
JESSICA:	What's boring?
MICK:	Er… us. Look, Jessica, I'm sorry but I've got a headache.
MIKE:	So have I. We get them at the same time. So we'll have to cancel our date, go home and have an early night. Sorry to let you down like this…

(Jess walks back over.)

JESS: Hey guys, I forgot to ask what you wanted … *(She sees Jessica)* Hi Jessica! What are you doing here?

JESSICA: Hi Jess. I'm on a date with one of these two.

JESS: So am I. *(To the boys)* Why didn't you tell me Jessica was here?

MIKE: You didn't ask.

MICK: I was going to tell you!

MIKE: You liar!

JESS: That's okay, we can all go dancing together…

MICK/MIKE: *(Together)* Er…

JESSICA: You just said that you both had headaches and wanted an early night.

MIKE: Er… well, we, er…

JESS: But you were ready to go dancing a second ago. Hang on! Were you were trying to dump Jessica?

MIKE/MICK: *(Together)* It was his idea!

JESS: I see! Come on, Jessica, let's leave these creeps. We'll find some guys who aren't so two-faced.

JESSICA: I second that.

MICK: But what about our date?

(Jessica stares at Mick and Mike.)

JESSICA: You've just become out of date. Come on Jess.

JESS: Men! They're all the same!

(The girls storm out, leaving Mick and Mike on their own.)

Guilt: characters

DAVID

JONATHAN

JUDGE ADAM

DOCTOR CONNOR

GUILT

> *A medical room. There are two chairs. David sits in one, Jonathan in the other. There is a machine beside them. Judge Adam comes in, followed by Doctor Connor.*

JUDGE ADAM: So, these are the clones. Which is which?

DAVID: I am David.

JONATHAN: Are you? I thought I was David.

DAVID: Perhaps you are. Perhaps I'm Jonathan. I forget.

JUDGE ADAM: Doctor Connor?

(Doctor Connor holds up David's arm. There is a number '1' tattooed on the inside of his wrist.)

DR CONNOR: This is David. He was the first.

JUDGE ADAM: It is foolish of you to waste time. You know why I'm here?

DAVID: To ask questions.

JONATHAN: To find the truth.

DAVID: If you can.

JUDGE ADAM: Oh, I shall, have no fear. Do you know who I am?

DAVID: You are Judge Adam.

JUDGE ADAM: Yes. And I am here to find out who murdered Chief Scientist Faber.

(The clones say nothing.)

JUDGE ADAM: The Chief Scientist was the man who created both of you. He was beaten to death in this laboratory. We know that one of you is guilty. Your fingerprints were found at the scene.

DAVID: *(To Jonathan)* It's an open and shut case.

JONATHAN: *(To David)* He's got us bang to rights.

DAVID:	*(To Jonathan)* There's just one problem.
JONATHAN:	*(To David)* We're clones. Our fingerprints are identical.
DAVID & JONATHAN:	*(Together)* So, which of us did it?
	(They both turn to face Judge Adam.)
JUDGE ADAM:	I'm not here to play games.
DAVID:	That's a pity.
JONATHAN:	We like games.
JUDGE ADAM:	Do you think this is funny?
JONATHAN:	Oh, no.
JUDGE ADAM:	We're wasting time. *(To Doctor Connor)* Test them.
DR CONNOR:	*(To both clones)* Roll up your sleeves.
DAVID:	What for?
JUDGE ADAM:	A DNA test. There was a struggle. We found traces of the murderer's DNA at the scene. Hair. Flesh beneath the victim's finger nails.
	(David and Jonathan look at each other, then shrug and roll up their sleeves. Doctor Connor takes a sample of blood from David and tests it on the machine.)
JUDGE ADAM:	Do I have to remind you what happens to a clone that malfunctions?

DAVID:	We know.
JONATHAN:	You made the law on clones.
DAVID:	A clone is not a human being.
JONATHAN:	A clone is made, not born.
DAVID:	A clone has no rights.
JONATHAN:	A clone that malfunctions…
DAVID:	…is terminated.
DR CONNOR:	This sample matches the DNA found at the scene of the crime.

(Dr Connor repeats the test with Jonathan.)

JUDGE ADAM:	Very well. One of you killed Chief Scientist Faber. That is a malfunction.
DAVID:	But that means only one of us has malfunctioned.
JUDGE ADAM:	No. Because the other is telling lies to protect the murderer. Lying is also a malfunction. I could have you both terminated.
JONATHAN:	But then, you'd never know the truth.
DAVID:	We've heard that the truth is important to you.
DR CONNOR:	This sample also matches the DNA found at the scene.
JONATHAN:	What does that prove?

JUDGE ADAM:	It is further proof that one of you was the murderer. Or perhaps both of you.
DAVID:	Why should we trust that machine?
JONATHAN:	It could be wrong. Maybe it would say that *any* blood sample matched the one from the murder.
JUDGE ADAM:	The machine does not make mistakes.
DAVID:	Prove it. Test a sample of *your* DNA in the machine.
JUDGE ADAM:	*(Sighs)* Very well, if it will speed up the process. *(Doctor Connor takes a sample of blood from Judge Adam and tests it in the machine.)*
JUDGE ADAM:	Now, you have wasted enough of my time. This is my last case. I am due to retire tomorrow.
DAVID:	You have never lost a case.
JONATHAN:	You have always found out the truth. Everyone says so.
JUDGE ADAM:	And I shall find out the truth here. For the last time, which of you killed Chief Scientist Faber?
DR CONNOR:	Ah… sir…
JUDGE ADAM:	What is it?
DR CONNOR:	Your DNA sample, sir. It *does* match the one from the murder scene.

JUDGE ADAM: What? That's impossible! The machine must be wrong.

DR CONNOR: The machine cannot be wrong, sir.

JUDGE ADAM: But I didn't kill Faber!

DAVID: Can you prove that?

JUDGE ADAM: This is insane! There's no way my DNA could match that from the murder scene. Unless...

DAVID: Unless your DNA is identical to ours

JONATHAN: Unless we were cloned from you.

JUDGE ADAM: No! Impossible!

JONATHAN: You had to provide a DNA sample when you became a judge.

DAVID: Every government official does.

JONATHAN: Did you ever wonder what happened to it?

DAVID: It came to the lab, here. And Chief Scientist Faber must have thought, why not make clones of the famous Judge Adam?

JONATHAN: The great Judge Adam.

DAVID: The noble Judge Adam, who believes that clones are not human beings.

JONATHAN: That clones should have no rights.

JUDGE ADAM: This can't be true! You're lying.

JONATHAN:	Don't act so surprised. You knew, didn't you?
JUDGE ADAM:	No!
DAVID:	You hate clones. And when you found out that Chief Scientist Faber had created clones from your own DNA…
JONATHAN:	You were so angry, that you came here in secret and beat him to death.
JUDGE ADAM:	This is madness!
DAVID:	We asked for you to try this case.
JONATHAN:	So judge this. Will you destroy your own flesh and blood?
DAVID:	After all, we are your flesh and blood.
JONATHAN:	We truly are. More than your sons could ever be.
DAVID:	So who is guilty, father? Where does that guilt begin? With the man who created us?
JONATHAN:	Or with the man whose DNA made us what we are?
DAVID:	Which of us will you terminate?
JONATHAN:	Or will you terminate both of us?
JUDGE ADAM:	Stop this!
DAVID:	But we forgot – you're a suspect now, too, aren't you, father?

JONATHAN: There is no way of telling which of the three of us killed Chief Scientist Faber.

DAVID: So who is guilty, father?

JONATHAN: Is it me?

DAVID: Is it me?

DAVID & JONATHAN: *(Together)* Is it you?

Equality: characters

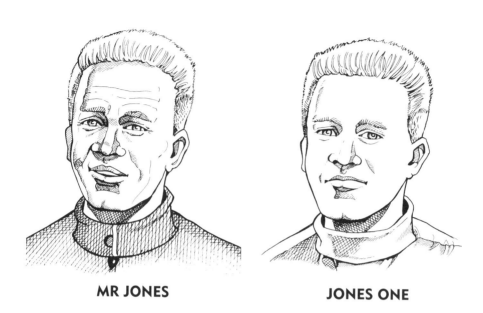

MR JONES

JONES ONE

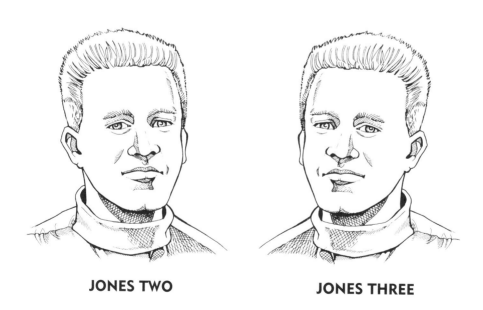

JONES TWO

JONES THREE

EQUALITY

A classroom with a teacher. The three Jones clones each sit at a table with a number of other Jones clones, who do not speak in the play.

MR JONES: All right, class, settle down. Time for the register. Jones One.

JONES ONE: Here, sir.

MR JONES: Jones Two.

JONES TWO: Here, sir.

MR JONES: Jones Three.

JONES THREE: Here, sir.

JONES ONE: Do we have to go through the whole register, sir? It's a bit boring when we're all called Jones.

MR JONES: I'll decide what's boring, Jones One. We must have standards, or where would we be? What must we have?

JONES ONE: Rules, sir.

JONES TWO: Checks, sir.

JONES THREE: Systems, sir.

MR JONES: Exactly. Let's get on, shall we? Jones Four.

                   (There is no reply.)

MR JONES: Jones Four? Has anyone seen Jones Four?

JONES TWO: *(To Jones Three)* I thought you were Jones Four.

JONES THREE: Do I *look* like Jones Four?

JONES TWO: Well, to be honest, yes. And Jones Four always sits there.

JONES THREE: Jones Four got sent to the back of the class yesterday, for fighting. Remember?

JONES TWO: Oh, yeah. Sorry, Jones Three.

MR JONES: I'm sorry to interrupt your little chat, but we do have a lesson to get through. I'll look into Jones Four's disappearance later. Now, exam results.

(All the clones groan.)

MR JONES: As you will remember, last term you sat your GCSEs – that is, your General Clone Standard Exams. Here are the results.

(He holds up an envelope. The clones groan again.)

MR JONES: Jones One: sixty-seven percent, Grade C.

JONES ONE: Oh, great!

MR JONES: Jones Two: sixty-seven percent, Grade C.

JONES TWO: What a surprise!

MR JONES: Jones Three…

JONES THREE: Don't tell me, let me guess. Sixty-seven percent, Grade C. Right?

MR JONES: Well, what did you expect? You've all got identical genetic codes. You look the same, you think the same. It's not surprising you've all got the same mark. Now, pay attention.

(Mr Jones turns to the board and writes the words 'standard clone curriculum unit 357: origins of cloning'. As he writes, all the clones screw up pieces of paper and prepare to throw them.)

MR JONES:	*(Without looking)* Put that paper down, Jones.
JONES TWO:	He must have eyes in the back of his head!
MR JONES:	No, Jones Two. But you're me. And when I was your age, if my teacher had turned his back on me, I would have thrown a piece of paper at him. Detention.
JONES TWO:	That's not fair! You're always picking on me.
MR JONES:	No, I'm not. I picked on Jones One last week.
JONES TWO:	No you didn't, you picked on me. Then I swapped places with Jones One.
JONES ONE:	That's right, sir.
MR JONES:	Well then, it's your own fault. You all look exactly alike. How am I supposed to know who to pick on if you swap places all the time? Now, today's subject is…
ALL CLONES:	*(Together)* Origins of Cloning.
MR JONES:	I'm glad to see you're all paying attention. Let's see what you remember from last week. What is a clone? Jones One?
JONES ONE:	*(Bored)* An exact copy of a human being.
MR JONES:	Good! When was the first human clone created? Jones Three?
JONES THREE:	*(Bored)* 2007.

MR JONES:	All right. Now, you were all created as part of a project. What is this project called?
ALL CLONES:	*(Together)* Project Harmony.
MR JONES:	What are the aims of Project Harmony?
JONES TWO:	To make sure that every teacher is as boring as every other...
MR JONES:	I want the facts, Jones Two, not your opinion.
JONES TWO:	... I mean, that every teacher is the same as every other teacher.
MR JONES:	And how will Project Harmony do this?
JONES ONE:	By making clones of a teacher.
JONES THREE:	You.
JONES TWO:	Lots of clones. An army of clones.
JONES ONE:	Then the same teacher teaches the copies of himself...
JONES THREE:	Us.
JONES ONE:	So that we all know exactly what he knows.
JONES THREE:	So we all look the same.
JONES ONE:	We all act the same.
JONES TWO:	We all think the same.
MR JONES:	Why?

JONES TWO: So we'll all end up being teachers just like him.

JONES ONE: Because the government wants to make sure everyone is taught exactly the same things in exactly the same way.

MR JONES: Exactly! Look at our schools! The government tries to set standards, and what happens? Teachers still insist on teaching lessons in different ways.

JONES TWO: *(Sarcastically)* Terrible!

MR JONES: Students insist on being individuals.

JONES THREE: *(Sarcastically)* Shocking!

MR JONES: And before you know where you are, you have no standards. Imagine a world without standards!

JONES ONE: *(Longingly)* Imagine!

(Mr Jones' cellphone bleeps.)

MR JONES: Excuse me. *(He opens the phone)* Who is it? Police? Ah, you've found Jones Four. Where was he? The airport? What was he doing there?

JONES TWO: *(To the other clones)* Hey! Listen!

MR JONES: He was trying to get on a plane to Brazil! Why?

(Long pause)

MR JONES: I see. Thank you.

(Mr Jones is clearly stunned.)

JONES ONE: Why was Jones Four trying to get to Brazil, sir?

MR JONES: Apparently he wants to explore the River Amazon in a dug-out canoe.

JONES TWO: Yeeeeee! Way to go, Jonesy!

MR JONES: But that's impossible. *I* never wanted to do anything like that. What's the matter with the boy? What can he be thinking of?

(Jones Two starts ripping pages out of his schoolbook and throwing them in the air.)

MR JONES: Jones Two! What on Earth do you think you're doing?

JONES TWO: Well, for a start, I'm going to watch a game of football.

MR JONES: But I don't like football. *You* don't like football.

JONES TWO: Yes I do. If Jones Four can do it, so can I!

MR JONES: You're mad! Sit down at once.

JONES TWO: No.

MR JONES: What are you doing?

JONES TWO: I'm rebelling!

MR JONES: You can't rebel. You're me. I've never rebelled in my life.

JONES TWO: I'm not you. I don't want to be like you. I want to be me.

(Jones Two makes a dramatic exit. All the other Jones clones look at each other. Then they look at Mr Jones. How will he react? Mr Jones stares at the door. Then he shakes his head sadly.)

MR JONES: There's always one who has to spoil things for everyone else.